THE NON-PROPHET'S GUIDE™ TO PROPHECY FOR YOUNG PEOPLE

Written & Illustrated by
TODD HAMPSON

HARVEST KIDS

HARVEST HOUSE PUBLISHERS
EUGENE, OREGON

Published in association with William K. Jensen Literary Agency, 119 Bampton Court, Eugene, Oregon 97404

Cover design by Bryce Williamson

Interior design by Chad Dougherty

For bulk, special sales, or ministry purchases, please call 1 (800) 547-8979.
Email: Customerservice@hhpbooks.com

The Non-Prophet's Guide™ to Prophecy for Young People
Text and artwork copyright © 2022 by Todd Hampson
Published by Harvest House Publishers
Eugene, Oregon 97408
www.harvesthousepublishers.com

ISBN 978-0-7369-8280-1 (pbk.)
ISBN 978-0-7369-8281-8 (eBook)

Library of Congress Control Number: 2021947860

Printed in the United States of America

22 23 24 25 26 27 28 29 30 / VP / 10 9 8 7 6 5 4 3 2 1

CONTENTS

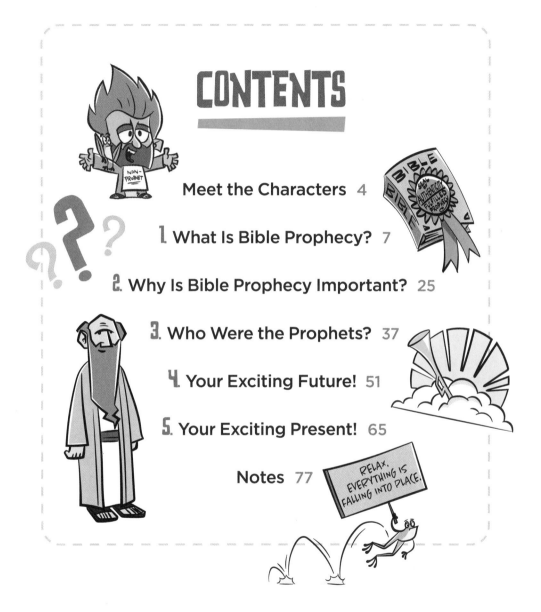

RELAX, EVERYTHING IS FALLING INTO PLACE.

MEET the

THE NON-PROPHET

Meet the Non-Prophet. He prefers the clothing, speech, food, facial grooming (or lack thereof), and customs of an Old Testament prophet, living in twenty-first-century America.

His eccentricities do not stop there, however. The Non-Prophet is also chronologically challenged. He often forgets what era he lives in, and his prophetic insights are ill-timed as he boldly proclaims things that have already occurred. There is one last thing you must know about the Non-Prophet. He is not wise with his money and doesn't understand that a freelancing Non-Prophet with no business acumen or marketable skills may struggle to make ends meet. He epitomizes the phrase "a day late and a dollar short." After misunderstanding prophecy, he may ask to borrow five bucks before he moves on to his next non-prophetic assignment.

CHARACTERS

MY NAME IS PLAGUE

PLAGUE

Plague is the Non-Prophet's pet frog. The Non-Prophet named him Plague after reading about the plague of frogs in chapter 8 of the book of Exodus. Despite his bad rap of being associated with a biblical plague, this frog is actually a great pet and rather harmless. Sometimes you'll see Plague off of his leash, but don't worry. He doesn't bite. In fact, he's quite intelligent and easy to get along with. He's actually the brains of the operation. Plague understands prophecy much better than the Non-Prophet, so keep an eye on him and the cues he provides throughout this book.

CHAPTER 1

WHAT IS BIBLE PROPHECY?

GUESS WHAT?

The Bible is the only religious book that has fulfilled prophecy or claims to be from God!

NON-PROPHET

> Remember the things I have done in the past. For I alone am God! I am God, and there is none like me. Only I can tell you the future before it even happens. Everything I plan will come to pass, for I do whatever I wish.
>
> **ISAIAH 46:9-10 NLT**

Have you ever seen a movie you loved so much you couldn't wait to see it again? Maybe you told your best friend about it so you could watch it together. Even though you knew ahead of time what was going to happen, you loved watching the movie with your friend. If this has happened to you, I bet it was really tough to resist telling them what was about to happen in each scene. When you're excited about what's to come, it's hard to keep it to yourself!

God is all-knowing, all-powerful, and eternal. Since he is all-knowing, God has foreknowledge of what is to come in the future. Also, we live moment-to-moment in what we refer to as time. God, on the other hand, is eternal. He is not limited by time or space. Think of it like this: We live life as if we were seeing a movie for the first time, but God sees all of history in advance—like a favorite movie he's already seen. Bible prophecy is really just history told in advance. You and I might read history books to learn what happened in the past. God sees the future as if it has already happened—as if it were already recorded in a history book! We can't fully understand how this works, but that's okay because we are not God. In fact, that's one of the reasons we worship God—he has qualities that are far beyond anything you and I can fully understand.

Definition

As you begin reading this book, let's begin with a working definition of what Bible prophecy is.

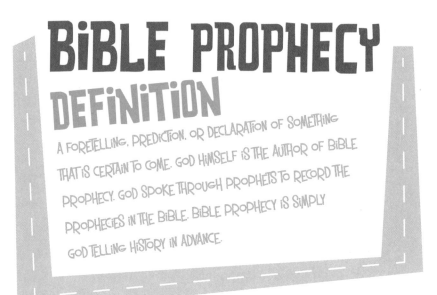

BIBLE PROPHECY DEFINITION

A FORETELLING, PREDICTION, OR DECLARATION OF SOMETHING THAT IS CERTAIN TO COME. GOD HIMSELF IS THE AUTHOR OF BIBLE PROPHECY. GOD SPOKE THROUGH PROPHETS TO RECORD THE PROPHECIES IN THE BIBLE. BIBLE PROPHECY IS SIMPLY GOD TELLING HISTORY IN ADVANCE.

Prediction Versus Prophecy

Have you ever heard someone make a prediction? Maybe a weather forecaster said it would rain the next day. Or perhaps a sportscaster was convinced that an underdog football team was going to win an upcoming game. Those are predictions, hunches, or educated guesses based on an analysis of facts and sometimes a gut feeling. Such predictions are impressive when they end up being correct, but often they are not. People's predictions are occasionally accurate, but they are never completely reliable—and

PREDICTION/FORECAST

BIBLICAL PROPHECY

they usually have very limited outcomes to choose from to begin with. For example, if two teams are playing each other and a sportscaster picks a winner, he has a 50/50 chance of being right.

A Bible prophecy, on the other hand, is very different from a human prediction. Many of the Bible's predictions were given hundreds or even thousands of years in advance and involve many specific details. Most of the prophecies in the Bible have already happened—and they have a 100 percent accuracy record! These prophecies are not just about topics with only a few possible outcomes, such as the weather or a sporting event. Instead, they contain mind-blowing details about important historical events, conditions, and people. Every time a Bible prophecy has been fulfilled, each detail of the prophecy has been accurate. If Bible prophecy were a baseball player, it would hit a home run every single time at bat!

Imagine that someone gave you a comic book with you as the main character. You're so excited, you read the whole book in one sitting, and you count ten things that happen to you in the comic book. Then as you go about your day, the things you just read about happen to you exactly like you read in the comic book and in exactly the same order. By the afternoon, eight of the ten events happened just as seen in the comic book. Do you think that would give you confidence the final two events would also happen to you? That's what Bible prophecy is like. Roughly 80 percent of the prophecies have already happened. The remaining 20 percent have to do with Jesus's return at the end of the age.

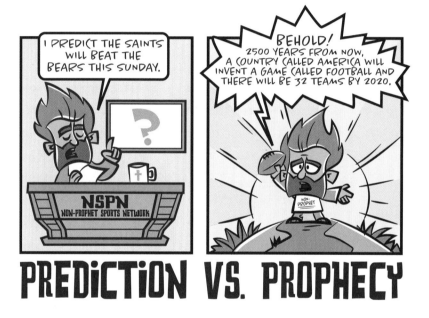

Note: This is not a prophecy from the Bible, but a way to show the difference between a prediction and a prophecy.

The Central Nervous System

Now let's take a look at how much prophecy is in the Bible. There are more than 31,000 verses in the Bible, and 9,000 to 10,000 of those verses contain specific predictions about future events. Experts say that between 27 and 33 percent of the Bible is prophecy. Roughly 7000 of the verses that contain Bible prophecy (about 80 percent) have already been fulfilled. The remaining 20 percent of the prophecies of the Bible will happen at some time in the future. That means we can watch for them. Isn't that exciting?

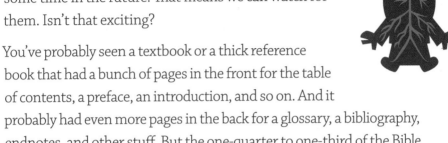

THE CENTRAL NERVOUS SYSTEM OF THE BIBLE

1/4 PROPHECY

80% FULFILLED

20% STILL FUTURE

You've probably seen a textbook or a thick reference book that had a bunch of pages in the front for the table of contents, a preface, an introduction, and so on. And it probably had even more pages in the back for a glossary, a bibliography, endnotes, and other stuff. But the one-quarter to one-third of the Bible made up of prophecy isn't fluff or bonus content—it's the most important part! Bible prophecy is like the central nervous system of the Bible.

Biologists study systems in organisms—the digestive system; the cardiovascular system; the muscular system, and so on. None of those systems can work without the central nervous system. They are all connected to it and rely on it. Just as living things like humans and animals can't function properly without a healthy central nervous system, the Bible can't be accurately understood without the all-important feature of prophecy.

All key teachings (doctrine and theology), stories, people, and themes in the Bible are somehow connected to Bible prophecy. It is the electric current that brings the Bible to life, separating it from any other book ever written! This is because the Bible (though penned by at least 39 human

Guess what?

The first prophecy in the Bible is found in Genesis 3:15. The last prophecy of the Bible is found in Revelation 22:20.

writers on three different continents over a period of 1500 years) was inspired by God.

Second Timothy 3:16 tells us that the Bible was "God-breathed." Second Peter 1:21 tells us that those who wrote prophecy "spoke from God" and were "carried along by the Holy Spirit." In other words. God told them what to write. That is why the whole Bible tells one complete story. This story is tied together by prophecy, and it all ultimately points to Jesus!

Now that you know what prophecy is, let's take a look at several amazing examples of fulfilled Bible prophecy.

Example 1—Prophecies About Jesus

During Christmas, you've probably seen a nativity scene depicting the birth of Jesus. We all know how special that moment was. Hundreds of years before Jesus was born in that manger, prophets recorded messages from God about the details of Jesus's birth, life, ministry, death, and resurrection.

These are known as *messianic prophecies* because they were prophecies about the coming Messiah. The word *messiah* means "anointed one," so people use the word to describe a savior or deliverer. The Old Testament foretold that a Savior was coming to save the Jewish people and the whole world!

The Bible includes more than 300 prophecies about the first coming of Jesus Christ. They include things like the virgin birth (Isaiah 7:14); where the Messiah would be born (Micah 5:2); what tribe he would come from (Genesis 49:10); that he would minister in Galilee (Isaiah 9:1-2); many details of his death, burial, and resurrection (Psalm 16:10; 22:16; 34:20; 41:9; Isaiah 50:6; 53:3-12; Zechariah 11:12-13); and lots of other facts.

In the early 1950s, a famous mathematician by the name of Peter Stoner wrote a book called *Science Speaks*. In this book, he calculated that for one person to fulfill just 8 of the more than 300 prophecies about Jesus's first coming would be as unlikely as the following scenario:

- **Mark a silver dollar with an X.**
- **Fill the state of Texas two feet deep with silver dollars.**
- **Randomly mix the single marked coin with the rest of the coins anywhere in the state.**
- **Blindfold a man and let him wander the state as long as he wants.**
- **Finally, give the blindfolded man one chance to reach in and pick up a coin.**

The chances of the man choosing the marked coin are the same as the chances of one man fulfilling just 8 of the prophecies about the Messiah. And there are more than 300! In other words, it is impossible for one man to fulfill more than 300 messianic prophecies by chance.

26 OF THE 300+ PROPHECIES OF THE 1ST COMING

PROPHECY	PREDICTION	FULFILLMENT
Isaiah 7:14	born of a virgin	Luke 1:26-53
Micah 5:2	born in Bethlehem	Matthew 2:1
Hosea 11:1	flight into Egypt...	Matthew 2:14
Jeremiah 31:15	to escape death	Matthew 2:16
Genesis 49:10	from the tribe of Judah	Luke 3:33
Isaiah 7:14	called Immanuel	Matthew 1:23
Isaiah 9:1-2	ministry in Galilee	Matthew 4:12-16
Zechariah 9:9	triumphal entry into Jerusalem	Matthew 21:1-11
Psalm 41:9	betrayed by a friend...	Matthew 26:20-25
Zechariah 11:12	for 30 pieces of silver	Matthew 26:15
Zechariah 11:13	money used for potter's field	Matthew 26:6-7
Isaiah 53:3	rejected by Jews	John 1:11
Psalm 35:11	falsely accused	Matthew 26:59-68
Isaiah 53:7	silent before accusers	Matthew 27:12-14
Isaiah 50:6	hit and spit on	Mark 14:65
Isaiah 53:4-5	suffered for others (us)	Matthew 8:16-17
Isaiah 53:12	crucified with robbers	Matthew 27:38
Psalm 22:16	hands and feet pierced	John 20:25
Psalm 34:20	bones not broken	John 19:33
Psalm 22:18	lots cast for clothes	John 19:23-24
Psalm 22:15	thirsted on the cross...	John 19:28
Psalm 69:21	and given vinegar	John 19:29
Psalm 22:1	"My God, why have you forsaken me?"	Matthew 27:46
Isaiah 53:9	buried in tomb of rich	Matthew 27:57-61
Psalm 16:10	resurrection	Matthew 28:9
Psalm 68:18	ascension	Luke 24:50-51

Example 2—Four World Empires

Have you ever heard of the Old Testament book of Daniel? Maybe you've heard the story about Daniel in the lion's den, or the story about Daniel's three friends who were thrown into a fiery furnace but survived. Daniel was a prophet (we'll talk more about him and the other prophets in chapter 3). As a matter of fact, most of the book of Daniel contains prophecies. Eight of the twelve chapters of Daniel contain prophecy, and six of those chapters deal specifically with end-time prophecies.

In Daniel chapter 2, King Nebuchadnezzar of Babylon had a strange dream about a giant gleaming statue. None of the king's wise men could tell the king what his dream was or what it meant, but God revealed the dream and the interpretation to Daniel.

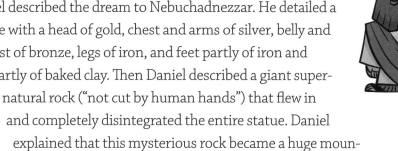

First, Daniel described the dream to Nebuchadnezzar. He detailed a statue with a head of gold, chest and arms of silver, belly and waist of bronze, legs of iron, and feet partly of iron and partly of baked clay. Then Daniel described a giant supernatural rock ("not cut by human hands") that flew in and completely disintegrated the entire statue. Daniel explained that this mysterious rock became a huge mountain that filled the earth.

After his description, Daniel interpreted the dream for Nebuchadnezzar (and us). As he did so, he provided a sweeping prophecy that accurately predicted four successive world empires and then leaped forward to the time of the end.

The four kingdoms represented by the various metals were the Babylonian Empire, the Medo-Persian Empire, the Greek Empire,

READ ABOUT iT!

DANiEL 2:39-45

and the Roman Empire. Daniel's prophecies about these four successive kingdoms (and many other prophecies in Daniel) are so accurate that critics used to say that Daniel had to be written after the fact. But then beginning in 1947 a game-changing discovery was made. Hundreds of ancient scrolls were found near the Dead Sea in Israel—including the book of Daniel. This discovery of the Dead Sea Scrolls would prove that the book of Daniel—including the accurate prophecies—had already been around for generations!

Several other very specific Old Testament prophecies regarding world events, nations, and people groups have been fulfilled. In Isaiah 44–45, God even predicted the then-future King Cyrus by name—150 years in advance! Imagine that!

IMAGINE THIS!

What if you picked up a book someone wrote 150 years ago and discovered a set of accurate prophecies in the book about your life—and it even had your name written in it!

Example 3—The People of Israel

In the Old Testament, a few hundred years after the flood of Noah's day, God picked a man named Abram and made some unconditional promises to him and changed his name to Abraham, which means "father of a multitude," or "father of many people." God promised Abraham that he would make a great nation out of his descendants. He also promised that everyone on earth would be blessed through him (through the Messiah, Jesus). As part of God's covenant, he promised to give

Abraham's descendants a very specific piece of land. It was known as the Promised Land. The heart of that land is what we know today as Israel (named after Abraham's grandson).

About 500 years after Abraham died, the Jewish leader Moses would lead more than two million of Abraham's descendants (600,000 men plus women and children, according to Exodus 12:37) out of Egypt, where they had been slaves for about 400 years. God then gave Moses instructions detailing how the Jewish people were to live as they traveled to the Promised Land and settled there. This was known as the Law.

Many of the details of the Law were recorded by Moses in the book of Deuteronomy. There we find some very specific prophecies about what would happen to the Jewish people (and the Promised Land) in the future if they obeyed God—and what would happen if they disobeyed God. One of the things Moses said would happen if they disobeyed God (by turning from him and worshipping false gods) was that they would be conquered and lose their land. They would be kicked out of the Promised Land and scattered all over the world for a long time.

Sadly, these prophesies also said that they would be severely mistreated in the nations where they would be scattered. Thankfully, the prophecies also said that

COVENANT MEANS "PROMiSE"

want to study more?

Read Genesis chapters 12, 13, 15, and 17 to learn all about God's covenant with Abraham.

GUESS what?

Jesus died for the sins of the world so that anyone who accepts his gift of salvation can be right with God again!

John 3:16 For God so loved the world that he gave his one and only Son, that whoever believes in him shall not perish but have eternal life.

God would preserve his people while they were away from their land. Finally, God said that after a long time, he would regather them back to their own land.

The scattering of the Jewish people is known in modern times as the Diaspora. In AD 70 the Romans attacked Jerusalem and killed more than 1 million Jewish people. This began the spread of the Jewish people into many other countries. The land of Israel eventually became known as Palestine. Israel had lost its country, and its people were scattered all over the world.

JEWISH DIASPORA
(ISRAEL'S DISPERSION)

1878 YEARS (AD 70-1948)

240+ YEARS
AGE OF AMERICA

The mistreatment of the Jewish people while away from their land is known in modern times as anti-Semitism. Just about everywhere the Jewish people went, they experienced severe anti-Semitism. This led many to settle in America, which (for the most part) has been friendly to the Jewish people.

ALIYAH
MEANS
"ASCENT"

AS IN, "GOING UP TO JERUSALEM,"
which is a higher elevation than the surrounding land. In the 1800s there were roughly 24,000 Jewish people in the land. Today there are almost 7 million![1]

The regathering of the Jewish people back to their homeland is known in modern times as aliyah. Each year many Jewish people not born in Israel change their citizenship to return to their homeland.

Roughly 2400 years ago, the Bible predicted that the Jewish people would be kicked out of their land, be scattered all over the earth for a long time, and then

would slowly but surely return to their original homeland. These prophecies have been stunningly fulfilled exactly as the Bible foretold!

Example 4—The Land of Israel

The Rebirth of a Nation

We've looked at some prophecies about the *people* of Israel, and we'll now look at some amazing prophecies about the *land* of Israel.

We often think of prophecy as being fulfilled in ancient times. If you will recall the section where we talked about the prophecies of Jesus's first coming, those prophecies were fulfilled almost 2000 years ago—long before cameras, film, digital video, or audio recordings were invented.

But what about in our day? Did you know that some prophecies have been fulfilled in amazing ways in modern times? You and I weren't around in 1948, but in that year one of the most mind-blowing prophesies of all time was fulfilled.

After almost 2000 years of there being no nation of Israel, the nation was reborn in a single day! This was exactly what prophecy foretold. Every Old Testament prophet except Jonah prophesied that Israel would become a nation again. Consider these verses written 2600 years ago:

- "'The days are coming,' declares the LORD, 'when it will no longer be said, "As surely as the LORD lives, who brought the Israelites up out of Egypt," but it will be said, "As surely as the LORD lives, who brought the Israelites up out of the land of the north and out of all the countries where he had banished them." For I will restore them to the land I gave their ancestors'" (Jeremiah 16:14-15).

- "I will take you out of the nations; I will gather you from all the countries and bring you back into your own land" (Ezekiel 36:24).

- "In that day the Lord will reach out his hand a second time to bring back the remnant of his people" (Isaiah 11:11 NLT).

- "Who has ever heard of such things? Who has ever seen things like this? Can a country be born in a day or a nation be brought forth in a moment? Yet no sooner is Zion in labor than she gives birth to her children" (Isaiah 66:8).

Notice two things. First, that this would be the second time Israel's people would return. (The first was after the Babylonian captivity in the sixth century BC.) Second, that the nation would be reborn in a single day. This is literally what happened. The last day of British oversight of the land was on May 14, 1948, and on the very same day the Declaration of the Establishment of the State of Israel was proclaimed. Israel was literally born in a day. A nation was brought forth in a moment!

A Land Brought Back to Life

The preservation of the Jewish people and the rebirth of the nation were clearly prophesied in Scripture. So was the fact that the land of Israel would remain a dry wasteland until the Jewish people returned.

In Ezekiel 36:34-35 we read, "The desolate land will be cultivated instead of lying desolate in the sight of all who pass through it. They will say, 'This land that was laid waste has become like the garden of Eden; the cities that were lying in ruins, desolate and destroyed, are now fortified and inhabited.'"

Have you ever heard of Mark Twain? His real name was Samuel Clemens, and he wrote books like *The Adventures of Tom Sawyer* and *The Adventures of Huckleberry Finn*. But he also wrote a book detailing his world travels. About 70 years before Israel became a nation again, Mark Twain explored the ancient land of Israel, and this is what he wrote:

> [A] desolate country...We never saw a human being on the whole route...There was hardly a tree or a shrub anywhere. Even the olive and the cactus, those fast friends of the worthless soil, had almost deserted the country.[2]

Once God's chosen people were back in God's chosen land, it burst back into life. Weather patterns changed, the land was cultivated, and now the cities and vegetation are flourishing. The former wasteland now generates so much produce that Israel exports fruit and vegetables to Europe! Just 70 years from its founding, the tiny nation of Israel has become the eighth most powerful nation in the world!

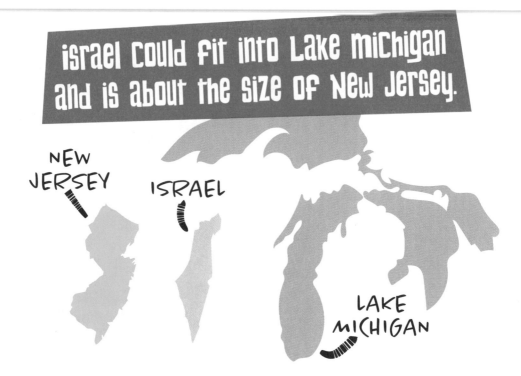

Now that you have a better idea of *what* Bible prophecy is, in the next chapter we're going to talk about *why* it is so important.

CHAPTER 2

WHY IS BIBLE PROPHECY IMPORTANT?

GUESS WHAT?

The Bible has a built-in seal of authenticity. Turn the page to find out more!

NON-PROPHET

> I foretold the former things long ago, my mouth announced them and I made them known; then suddenly I acted, and they came to pass.
>
> ## ISAIAH 48:3

Today, you and I can turn on the TV or search online in the comfort of our living rooms to see exotic animals from all over the world—monkeys, tigers, Komodo dragons, narwhals, duck-billed platypuses, whale sharks, and silverback gorillas. You name it, you can find it online. But it wasn't always that way. Before modern inventions such as cameras, digital video, or audio recording technology, explorers had to draw or describe the amazing creatures they encountered.

Before 1806, when Lewis and Clark returned from their famous expedition into the western portion of the United States, nobody in the scientific community even knew that grizzly bears, prairie dogs, coyotes, jack rabbits, or pronghorns

existed. Lewis and Clark discovered at least 122 animals that were new to science![3] They had heard stories from Native American Indians about 1000-pound bears but were skeptical—until a grizzly bear tried to eat Lewis!

Lewis and Clark brought home journals filled with descriptions, drawings, and stories of their encounters with these newly discovered animals, yet some people didn't believe all their accounts of new animal discoveries. Over time, all of their animal discoveries were verified by other eyewitness accounts and westward expansion, but first others had to take their word for it.

Evidence the Bible Is from God

When we consider the amazing truths of the Bible, we accept them by faith. We believe in the Trinity—the three-in-one God of the universe. We believe Jesus was the Son of God sent here to die for our sins. We believe he was resurrected on the third day. We believe that if we place our trust in Jesus, we receive God's grace, our sins are forgiven, and we are born again spiritually!

These are amazing truths that we accept by faith. In fact, Hebrews 11:6 says, "Without faith it is impossible to please God." We get right with God through faith. But here's the question: Is it a blind faith or a faith that's based on evidence? I'll answer that in a moment, but first let's talk about the difference between proof and evidence.

Proof is undeniable. Some people may not have believed Lewis and Clark's description of a grizzly bear, but if the explorers brought back an actual grizzly bear to show the people, they could prove it. Instead, the people had to rely on evidence, such as the eyewitness accounts of Lewis and Clark and their crew, the drawings, the hair samples, and the journal descriptions.

We don't have a photograph of God, and we don't have a video of God writing the Bible, so we accept these things by faith. But it is faith based on evidence. There's a special name for the study of evidence that demonstrates God is real and the Bible is true—it's called *apologetics*. Apologetics doesn't mean we apologize for something. The term comes from the ancient Greek word *apologia*, which means "to make a reasoned defense of something."

APOLOGETICS
DEFINITION

The term comes from the ancient Greek word **apologia** which means "to make a reasoned defense of something."

One of the strongest apologetics, or evidences, that the Bible is from God is that it contains so many prophecies that have been fulfilled. The fact that the Bible has hundreds of very detailed prophecies that have come to pass exactly as they were foretold serves as very strong evidence that the Bible is from God. Fulfilled prophecy is the Bible's built-in seal of authenticity.

The Bible claims to be the Word of God and backs up this claim with fulfilled Bible prophecy. Many people don't realize this, but no other religion-founding book has either of these features. Look what God said in Isaiah 46:9-10:

> Remember the former things, those of long ago; I am God, and there is no other; I am God, and there is none like me. I make known the end from the beginning, from ancient times, what is still to come. I say, "My purpose will stand, and I will do all that I please."

After Jesus told his disciples that he was returning to the Father, he added this: "I have told you now before it happens, so that when it does happen you will believe" (John 14:29). So some of the purposes of prophecy are to provide evidence the Bible is from God and to help us believe all the other things taught in Scripture! We've never seen heaven or Jesus, but the evidence we *can* see (fulfilled Bible prophecy) helps us trust God with the things we *can't* see (heaven, the rapture, and so on).

Evidence God Is a Promise-Keeper

A man's word is his bond. This short but powerful phrase from a past generation highlights the importance of keeping your word. If you say

you are going to do something, then do it. Or as the Bible puts it, "Let your 'Yes' be 'Yes,' and your 'No,' 'No.' For whatever is more than these is from the evil one" (Matthew 5:37 NKJV).

Has someone made a promise to you that they didn't keep? How did that make you feel? Did you feel like you could trust any other promises they made? Probably not. When someone breaks a promise, we lose trust in their words. Likewise, if someone consistently keeps their promises, we gain trust in their words. Their track record of keeping or breaking promises helps us decide whether to trust the other things they say.

We can be thankful that we serve a God who always keeps his promises. The fact that we have hundreds of fulfilled prophecies from the Bible should give us great confidence that all of God's promises will come true. God has given us hundreds of promises for this life and the next. We can trust these amazing promises because he has proven that his word is his bond.

Evidence That Future Prophecy Will Be Fulfilled

Just as we can trust that God will keep his promises, we can also trust that the prophecies that haven't been fulfilled yet will be fulfilled in the future. All of the prophecies that haven't been fulfilled yet are about the end times. We are currently in the time period known as the church age, or the age of grace.

BASIC ORDER
OF KEY END-TIME EVENTS

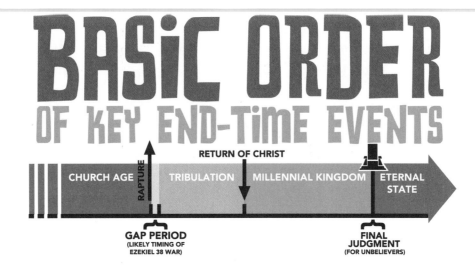

RETURN OF CHRIST

| CHURCH AGE | RAPTURE | TRIBULATION | MILLENNIAL KINGDOM | ETERNAL STATE |

GAP PERIOD
(LIKELY TIMING OF
EZEKIEL 38 WAR)

FINAL
JUDGMENT
(FOR UNBELIEVERS)

There are some very exciting prophecies that God has promised will happen in the future. Right now, this world can sometimes be a scary place. You may have lived through a tough time, or perhaps you've seen something on the news that made you fearful. Or maybe you've heard your parents talking about something scary in the world today.

In the future, God is going to set everything straight, punish all evil, and get rid of all of the scary stuff! The prophecies of the Bible that have not yet been fulfilled give us many amazing details about this future time period (and what heaven will be like). Since God has a 100 percent track record of fulfilling prophecy exactly as foretold, we can be confident that all future prophecy will be literally and accurately fulfilled at just the right time!

Here are some of the events the Bible says are going to happen. Remember, we can trust that these will all take place as

foretold in Scripture because all of the previous prophecies were fulfilled exactly as God said they would be. So no matter how "out there" or sensational some of these things sound, the Bible says they will happen literally and at God's appointed time.

The Rapture

The rapture is an amazing event that will take place at the end of the church age. Christians who have died will be resurrected, and we who are alive will join them to meet the Lord in the clouds. We read about it in 1 Thessalonians 4:13-18.

The Tribulation Period

The tribulation is the seven-year period of history that will take place after the rapture and before Christ's return to earth. This will be a period of judgment against evil world rulers and people who rebel against God. It will also be a time when many will turn to the Lord. We first learn of this seven-year period in Daniel chapter 9. We discover many more details about it in the book of Revelation, chapters 6 through 19. Though the judgments during this period sound very scary, we who know the Lord will not have to face this time of God's wrath.

Meanwhile, in Heaven

Once the church is taken to heaven in the rapture, we will all appear before the Bema Seat of Christ. This event will be like an Olympic medal ceremony—we will receive heavenly rewards (see 1 Corinthians 9:24-25). All who have accepted Christ as Savior are saved by grace. We can't work our way into heaven or be good enough to get there on our own. Only Jesus's substitutionary death on our behalf can pay for our sins and make us right with God. But once we are saved, we choose how we will live for the Lord. The Bema Seat is where our motives and opportunities to serve the Lord on earth will be evaluated. Second Corinthians 5:10 tells us, "We must all appear before the judgment seat of Christ, so that each of us may receive what is due us for the things done while in the body, whether good or bad."

After this amazing event, we will attend a banquet that the Bible calls the marriage supper of the Lamb. We read about this in Revelation 19:6-9. The church (which includes all true believers in Jesus) is referred to in the Bible as the bride of Christ. And Jesus is referred to as the Groom. The Bema Seat will be similar to the bride getting ready for the wedding. The marriage supper will be a big celebration to commemorate the marriage. We (the bride) will never have to face sin or death again, and our salvation will be complete. We will always be with Jesus. Since he is a promise-keeper, all of that is as good as done now—but one day it will be completely finished!

The Return of Christ

After the events in heaven and at the end of the tribulation period on earth, Jesus will leave heaven and physically come down to earth to defeat an evil ruler called the antichrist and his evil armies. Here's the cool part—we will be riding heavenly horses and gliding through the air behind Jesus as part of the heavenly armies! We will be in our new heavenly bodies, riding side by side with millions of angels.

The Millennial Kingdom

After Jesus defeats the evil armies, he will cast the evil world ruler and his evil false prophet into the Lake of Fire. Then God will cleanse the earth of corruption and set up a 1000-year kingdom on earth. During this time Jesus will rule from Jerusalem, and you and I who know Jesus will rule and reign with him! Satan will be bound at this time, but he will be let loose at the end of the 1000 years for one final battle—which he will lose quickly. Finally, God will cast Satan into the Lake of Fire forever. You can read about the millennial kingdom in Revelation 20:1-10 and in many of the prophets (more on that in the next chapter).

Eternity in Heaven

After the final battle, God will create a new heaven and a new earth. We will live in a place called the New Jerusalem. All evil will be gone, and we will live in perfect peace with everyone as we explore the universe, praise God for his holiness, and spend forever in an absolutely perfect situation with God in heaven.

Draw one small dot in the upper left-hand corner of the space below. Now draw one continuous squiggly line all around the rest of the square, filling up as much of the space as possible.

The dot represents your life on earth. The line represents eternity. In actuality, the line would never end! That is how long we'll be with the Lord! Knowing that this life is just a speck compared to how long we'll be with the Lord in heaven should help us live with more purpose and excitement about the things to come!

We'll talk much more about your amazing future in chapter 4, and we'll go into more detail about what heaven will be like. But first, let's learn who the prophets were and how God spoke through them so we could learn about all of the amazing things God foretold.

CHAPTER 3

WHO WERE THE PROPHETS?

GUESS WHAT?

Deuteronomy 18:22 · Prophets had to be right 100% of the time or they were disqualified!

NON-PROPHET

> We also have the prophetic message as something completely reliable, and you will do well to pay attention to it, as to a light shining in a dark place, until the day dawns and the morning star rises in your hearts. Above all, you must understand that no prophecy of Scripture came about by the prophet's own interpretation of things. For prophecy never had its origin in the human will, but prophets, though human, spoke from God as they were carried along by the Holy Spirit.
>
> ## 2 PETER 1:19-21

One of my favorite games in elementary school was telephone—you know, the game where the whole group sits in a circle and one person is given a message to whisper to the person next to them. Then each person whispers the message to the next person until the message has traveled all the way around the circle. The last person says the message out loud, and everyone cracks up laughing. Why? Because by the time the message gets to the last person, the original message has always been turned into some nonsensical and hilarious jumbled mess. The original message is always lost, rarely sounding anything like what was originally stated.

HA HA HA HA

RIBBIT RIBBIT RIBBIT CROAK!

NON-PROPHET

Definition

Fortunately, that is not the case with Bible prophecy. As we have seen, the accuracy of Bible prophecy proves its reliability. We are told by the apostle Peter (in the verses above) that the prophetic message is "completely reliable." Then he goes on to explain how the message of prophecy was delivered to us. He points out that the message didn't come from the prophets' own ideas, but directly from God. So who were these prophets, and what did they foretell? Let's find out!

PROPHET
DEFiNiTiON

a person chosen to speak for God, guide the people of israel, or record prophecies about God's activity including future, end-time events.

In the Old Testament, some prophets heard directly from God, like Noah, Abraham, and Moses. Joseph and Daniel interpreted dreams about prophecy. Elijah and Elisha were well-known prophets. Several prophets in the Old Testament wrote their own books (see below).

There were prophets in the New Testament too. John the Baptist was a prophet who lived in the desert and ate bugs (locusts to be exact) and wild honey. Simeon was an elderly prophet who knew he would see the Messiah before he died, and Anna was an elderly prophetess who worshipped at the temple awaiting the Messiah. Both of them got to see Jesus as a baby!

Peter and Paul were prophets and foretold future events. So was Jude. The most famous prophet of the New Testament is John. He was Jesus's closest disciple, and he wrote the final book of the Bible—Revelation.

The Period of the Prophets

During one period of about 300 years in Israel's ancient history, God sent several prophets to call Israel to turn back to the Lord. They recorded the prophecies in books bearing their names. The books of the prophets are arranged into two categories—the major prophets and the minor prophets. This doesn't mean some were more important than others, but that the major prophets wrote longer books than the minor prophets.

The prophets recorded prophecies about the near future as well as many prophecies about the end times. These are known as the mountain peaks of Bible prophecy. As the prophets foretold the future, they didn't always know how much time was in between the mountain peaks. They just recorded what they were told and sometimes didn't even know what their prophecies were all about. For example, on more than one occasion Daniel was confused about some prophecies and was told that some of them were rolled up and sealed until the time of the end (Daniel 12:4-9).

By the time of the prophets, the nation of Israel had split into two kingdoms: The northern kingdom kept the name Israel, and the southern kingdom was named after its largest tribe, Judah. Some prophets were in Israel and some were in Judah. Others, such as Ezekiel and Daniel, were taken away from their country as captives.

Obadiah 1 chapter
Isaiah 66 chapters

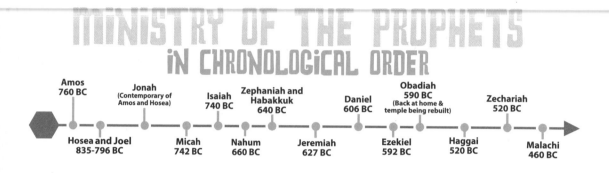

MINISTRY OF THE PROPHETS
IN CHRONOLOGICAL ORDER

Above the line	
Amos 760 BC	Jonah (Contemporary of Amos and Hosea)	Isaiah 740 BC	Zephaniah and Habakkuk 640 BC	Daniel 606 BC	Obadiah 590 BC (Back at home & temple being rebuilt)	Zechariah 520 BC

Below the line	
Hosea and Joel 835-796 BC	Micah 742 BC	Nahum 660 BC	Jeremiah 627 BC	Ezekiel 592 BC	Haggai 520 BC	Malachi 460 BC

First, let's look at the major prophets.

Major Prophets

Isaiah

Isaiah called Judah to repent and turn back to God. Isaiah wrote a lot about the redemptive work of the coming Messiah (Jesus). Isaiah 53, for example, is a clear depiction of the cross of Christ long before Rome came to power and started crucifying criminals. Isaiah also includes many prophecies of events that haven't happened yet, such as the future tribulation period and the glorious future kingdom (but more on that in chapter 4)!

ISAIAH

Isaiah's 66 chapters have two distinct sections—the first 39 chapters are mostly warnings about judgment, and the last 27 chapters are mostly about hope in the Messiah. That's a lot like the Bible, which has 66 books. Its 39 Old Testament books demonstrate the need for a Messiah, and its 27 books in the New Testament demonstrate the hope found in the Messiah.

Jeremiah

Jeremiah was known as the weeping prophet. He had a tough assignment. Jeremiah spent his whole life warning Judah to turn back to God because judgment was coming. Judah didn't listen, and the country was attacked and destroyed by the Babylonians. Jeremiah also wrote the book of Lamentations. A lament is an expression of grief or sorrow.

JEREMIAH

Ezekiel

Ezekiel prophesied during Judah's exile in Babylon. Ezekiel had an incredible vision of God's mobile throne in heaven. He also provided many prophecies about the future millennial kingdom (you'll learn about that in the next chapter) and had an amazing vision of God's throne room.

Daniel

DANIEL

Like Ezekiel, Daniel was a prophet while in captivity away from his homeland. Daniel recorded a lifetime of events and prophesies while in Babylon. Half of Daniel's book records historical events of his life. The other half is all prophecy. These are some of the key events recorded in Daniel:

EZEKIEL

- **He refused to eat the king's delicacies.**
- **His friends were thrown into a fiery furnace but survived unscathed.**
- **He was thrown into a den of hungry lions and survived unharmed.**

And here are just a few of the topics in Daniel's key prophecies:

- **Four world kingdoms (we met them in chapter 1 of this book)**
- **An end-time evil ruler**
- **Seventy weeks (of years) in Israel's future**
- **End-time events**

Minor Prophets

Hosea

Hosea wrote about God's unfailing love for Israel even though Israel disobeyed. Hosea was a prophet to the northern kingdom (Israel) and called the people to stop being unfaithful to God.

Joel

Joel was a prophet to Judah (the southern kingdom). During a time of great drought and a massive locust plague, Joel told the people they were experiencing judgment from God. He

JOEL

also pointed out that the locusts depicted an army that would attack in the future Day of the Lord (also known as the tribulation period)—a specific end-time period of God's judgment. Though this is a small book, it contains Joel's words for his time as well as powerful end-time prophecies.

Amos

Amos was from the southern kingdom (Judah) but preached in the northern kingdom (Israel). He was a shepherd who stood up for the poor and called the people back to God. He pointed out their evil practices and warned them to stop sinning before it was too late.

AMOS

Obadiah

The book of Obadiah is only one chapter long. It is a prophecy against the Edomites, who helped the Babylonians loot Jerusalem, the capital of the southern kingdom. Even though God allowed Judah to be conquered for disobedience, He wasn't going to let those who attacked his chosen people off the hook. Ancient Edom was in the area of southern Jordan.

OBADIAH

Jonah

God sent Jonah to tell the wicked city Nineveh, the capital of Assyria, to repent. Jonah said no and ran the opposite direction, but God used a special means of transportation to get him back to where he called Jonah to go. Surprisingly, the people of Nineveh repented and were not destroyed.

JONAH

Micah

Micah was a prophet to the southern kingdom (Judah). He preached to everyday people instead of to rulers.

MICAH

Nahum

Nahum prophesied against Nineveh about 100 years after Jonah did. The people of Nineveh repented after Jonah's preaching, but then they turned bad again. Nahum's basic message was, "Nineveh is going to be destroyed!"

NAHUM

Habakkuk

Habakkuk is a book of questions about evil in the world. Though Habakkuk was perplexed, his book helps people see how God is good and sovereign even though evil exists in the world. One day, God will set everything straight.

HABAKKUK

Zephaniah

Zephaniah was a prophet to Judah who warned of coming judgment. Like many other prophets, he prophesied about events that were soon to befall Israel and also about God's judgment in the future Day of the Lord.

ZEPHANIAH

Haggai

The nation of Judah was returning from 70 years of captivity in Babylon, and the people were beginning to rebuild again. Haggai encouraged the people to finish rebuilding the temple now that they were back in their land.

HAGGAI

Zechariah

Zechariah also prophesied to people returning to the land, encouraging them to finish building the new temple. He prophesied about Jesus coming

ZECHARIAH

the first time and again in the end times. Even though Zechariah is one of the smaller prophetic books (the minor prophets), he predicted more about the Messiah than any other prophet except Isaiah.

Malachi

Malachi used a question-and-answer method to call the people of Judah back to true worship and repentance instead of outward shows of piety. Though people were returning to the land, they were not all returning to God. Malachi is the last book of the Old Testament. The last word in the book of Malachi is "curse." After this prophet, there was no recorded Scripture that made it into the Bible for about 400 years!

MALACHI

Revelation 19:10 tells us, "It is the Spirit of prophecy who bears testimony to Jesus." In other words, the Holy Spirit worked through prophecy to point us to Jesus! As the Old Testament prophets fulfilled their calling in their day, God's bigger plan for them was to deliver prophecies about the first and second coming of Jesus.

Some people say that a golden thread runs through the Bible from Genesis to Revelation, and it leads to Jesus. In Luke 24:27 we're told, "Beginning with Moses and all the Prophets, [Jesus] explained to them what was said in all the Scriptures concerning himself."

Jesus is the central feature in all of Scripture, and every book in the Bible points to him. Next, let's talk about your amazing future!

CHAPTER 4

YOUR EXCITING FUTURE!

You can't even imagine how cool heaven is going to be.

GUESS what?

NON-PROPHET

> No eye has seen, no ear has heard, and no mind has imagined what God has prepared for those who love him.
>
> ## 1 CORINTHIANS 2:9 NLT
>
> Think about the things of heaven, not the things of earth.
>
> ## COLOSSIANS 3:2 NLT

This world is an amazing place with lots of fun things to do. But it is also a world where tough, sad, or scary things sometimes happen. The Bible teaches that one day, all of the bad stuff will be gone, and we will live with God forever in an adventure that lasts forever. Isn't that exciting?

If you have put your trust in Jesus for salvation, you have several mind-blowingly epic events in your future! Remember, about 80 percent of the prophecies in the Bible have already been fulfilled exactly as foretold. That means we can trust what God says about our future. I mention that because everything we're about to look at in this chapter sounds too good to be true, but it absolutely is!

The Rapture

First, we can look forward to an incredible event known as the rapture of the church. Imagine living a normal day...and then suddenly you hear some heavenly sounds—a shout, an angelic voice, a heavenly trumpet—and then *whoosh!* You are taken up in an instant, flying through the air like a superhero. As you fly into the clouds, you are joined by Christians from all over the world. Christians who have died years ago are there, hugging each other and reuniting with their loved ones who were still alive. Most amazingly, Jesus is there in all his brilliance. He is glowing and majestic. His eyes are shining, and dazzling heavenly light surrounds him. Yet he knows you and looks at you with compassion, joy, and perfect love.

The clearest description of this amazing future event is found in 1 Thessalonians chapter 4. There we learn that the final generation of Christians will not experience death, but will be taken suddenly to be with Jesus.

> According to the Lord's word, we tell you that we who are still alive, who are left until the coming of the Lord, will certainly not precede those who have fallen asleep. For the Lord himself will come down from heaven, with a loud command, with the voice of the archangel and with the trumpet call of God, and the dead in Christ will rise first. After that, we who are still alive and are left will be caught up together with them in the clouds to meet the Lord in the air. And so we will be with the Lord forever. Therefore encourage one another with these words (1 Thessalonians 4:15-18).

The Greek word translated "caught up" is *harpazō*, and it means...

- **to seize or carry off by force**
- **to seize on or eagerly claim for oneself**
- **to snatch out or away**

We also learn from Paul's writing to the believers in Corinth that this is the moment when God will instantly create our new, imperishable bodies. That means in heaven our new bodies will never age or wear out, and they will be able to do all sorts of new things in heaven.

> We will all be changed—in a flash, in the twinkling of an eye, at the last trumpet. For the trumpet will sound, the dead will be raised imperishable, and we will be changed (1 Corinthians 15:51-52).

Paul told the believers that we should look forward to the rapture and encourage one another about it! In 1 Thessalonians 5:10-11 we read, "He died for us so that, whether we are awake or asleep, we may live together with him. Therefore encourage one another and build each other up, just as in fact you are doing."

The rapture will happen at the end of the current church age, before a time of judgment known as the tribulation period. The church age is also known as the age of grace. *Grace* means "undeserved favor." In other words, now is a time when God offers to pay for our sins through faith in Jesus. He doesn't force anyone to accept his gift, but he is very patient and waits a long time so people have the opportunity to turn to God and avoid any judgment. At the end of this long period of grace, God must judge evil. Every good and righteous judge must eventually punish evil. God will do so during the future tribulation period. But those of us who know Jesus will go to be with him first. Because, as the two following verses tell us, Christians are "not appointed to wrath."

- **"God did not appoint us to suffer wrath but to receive salvation through our Lord Jesus Christ" (1 Thessalonians 5:9).**

- **"Since you have kept my command to endure patiently, I will also keep you from the hour of trial that is going to come on the whole world to test the inhabitants of the earth" (Revelation 3:10).**

That is why Paul said we should encourage each other (1 Thessalonians 5:11 above) with the news of the rapture!

Your Custom-Built Living Space

In the New Testament, Jesus, Paul, and others used the ancient Jewish wedding traditions to explain the relationship between Jesus and the church, which includes all true Christians. In these ancient Jewish wedding traditions, the groom would ask for permission to marry his potential bride. If the bride said yes, the groom paid her father a set price (since a valuable daughter would be leaving her family). At this point the man and woman were legally bound, but the groom would then go back to his father's house and build a custom living space for his bride. This would take a fairly long time. During the groom's absence, the bride would remain faithful and ready for the day her groom would come back.

jewish wedding traditions

PHASE 1 — ENGAGEMENT
- LEAVE FATHER'S HOUSE
- TRAVEL TO DESIRED BRIDE'S HOME
- PAY A GREAT PRICE FOR THE BRIDE
- OFFER ACCEPTED OR REJECTED
- MARRIAGE CONTRACT/LEGALLY BOUND TOGETHER
- GROOM BACK TO FATHER'S HOUSE TO PREPARE HOME

PHASE 2 — MARRIAGE
- FATHER SENDS SON BACK WHEN ALL IS READY
- GROOMSMEN ANNOUNCE GROOM'S ARRIVAL
- BRIDE IMMEDIATELY TAKEN BACK WITH GROOM
- THE TWO ENTER WEDDING CHAMBER FOR 7 DAYS
- GREAT WEDDING FEAST AT END OF 7 DAYS

Once the groom's father saw that the living space was ready and that the bride had remained faithful, he would send his son to fetch his bride at night. Though everyone knew the general timeframe, only the father knew the exact day and hour he would send his son.

The reason Jesus came the first time was to ask us to follow him. If we say yes, then his death on the cross satisfies the payment for our sins. He has gone back to his Father's house to build our custom living space. One day, when the Father knows the time is right, he will send his Son to come get us, and we will be raptured to meet him in the air. Remember, the church is also known as "the bride of Christ." The rapture is the moment when the heavenly groom (Jesus) comes to get his prepared bride (the church).

jewish wedding traditions
and the return of Christ

BETROTHAL	LEAVE FATHER'S HOUSE	JESUS LEFT HEAVEN
	TRAVEL TO DESIRED BRIDE'S HOME	CAME TO EARTH AS A BABY
	PAY A GREAT PRICE FOR THE BRIDE	DIED ON THE CROSS FOR OUR SINS
	OFFER ACCEPTED OR REJECTED	OFFERS SALVATION TO US
	MARRIAGE CONTRACT/LEGALLY BOUND TOGETHER	IF WE ACCEPT WE BECOME THE CHURCH ("BRIDE OF CHRIST")
	GROOM BACK TO FATHER'S HOUSE TO PREPARE HOME	JESUS WENT BACK TO PREPARE A PLACE FOR US

1ST COMING OF CHRIST

WEDDING	FATHER SENDS SON BACK WHEN ALL IS READY	GOD KNOWS THE "DAY AND HOUR" HE WILL SEND THE SON
	GROOMSMEN ANNOUNCE GROOM'S ARRIVAL	THE ARCHANGEL WILL SHOUT AND A TRUMPET WILL BLOW
	BRIDE IMMEDIATELY TAKEN BACK WITH GROOM	THE CHURCH/BRIDE OF CHRIST WILL BE RAPTURED
	THE TWO ENTER WEDDING CHAMBER FOR 7 DAYS	THE CHURCH WILL BE IN HEAVEN DURING THE TRIBULATION
	GREAT WEDDING FEAST AT END OF 7 DAYS	THE CHURCH WILL ATTEND THE WEDDING FEAST OF THE LAMB

RAPTURE AND CHURCH IN HEAVEN DURING TRIBULATION PERIOD

In John 14:2-3 Jesus said, "My Father's house has many rooms; if that were not so, would I have told you that I am going there to prepare a place for you? And if I go and prepare a place for you, I will come back and take you to be with me that you also may be where I am."

God created you and knows everything about you. You will still be you in heaven but with a new, eternal body that will be able to do amazing things. It will be like having superpowers, and your custom-built living space will be prepared just for you. If you like skateboarding, maybe you'll have a ten-mile skateboard track with loops and giant hills. If you like swimming, maybe you'll have an air-pool where you can swim in midair, or maybe you'll be able to breathe underwater. If you like art, maybe you'll be able to create glowing art with your hands on the walls or

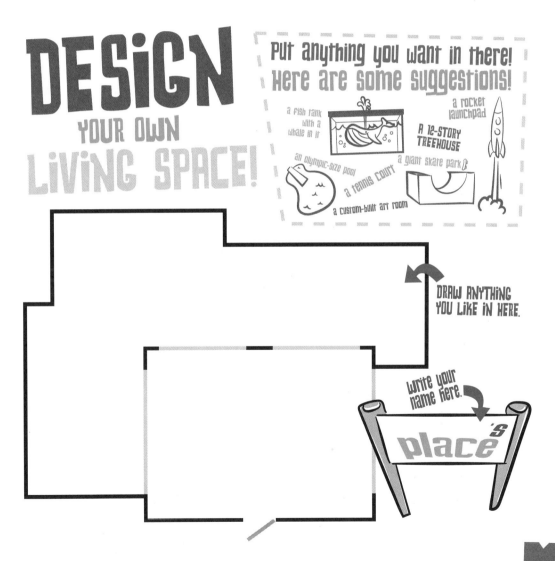

DESIGN YOUR OWN LIVING SPACE!

Put anything you want in there! Here are some suggestions!

a fish tank with a whale in it

a rocket launchpad

A 12-STORY TREEHOUSE

an olympic-size pool

a tennis court

a giant skate park

a custom-built art room

DRAW ANYTHING YOU LIKE IN HERE.

Write your name here.

's place

in midair. If you like gymnastics, maybe you'll have a high-bar apparatus with 100 bars that you'll be able to flip, swing, and bounce around on.

We don't know what our custom living areas will be like, but they are going to be amazing. God created everything we see in six days, so can you imagine how breathtaking our living spaces are going to be since he's been building them for almost 2000 years?

A Thousand-Year Kingdom

When we are kids, we love stories about a nice king ruling a vast kingdom and caring for his people. Maybe you've read the Chronicles of Narnia series, or *The Three Musketeers*, or the story of Robin Hood. Or maybe you've seen movies about a good king trying to rule his kingdom. This makes a great storyline because it is built into us as humans. Something in us knows that a perfect King ruling a vast kingdom is in our future.

During the seven-year tribulation period on earth, we as Christians will be enjoying some incredible planned events in heaven—including exploring our custom-built living spaces. After the tribulation period, we will return with Christ to earth, where he will immediately punish his enemies and then set up a 1000-year kingdom on earth in order to fulfill many Old Testament prophecies.

I saw an angel coming down out of heaven, having the key to the Abyss and holding in his hand a great chain. He seized the dragon, that ancient serpent, who is the devil, or Satan, and bound him for a thousand years. He threw him into the Abyss, and locked and

> sealed it over him, to keep him from deceiving the nations anymore until the thousand years were ended. After that, he must be set free for a short time (Revelation 20:1-3).

Many of the prophets we met in chapter 3 foretold a time when a descendant of David would rule the world with perfect righteousness from Jerusalem. It would be a golden age with no war, no deception, and no evil lurking behind the scenes. The land of the world would be reconfigured so everyone could easily travel to Jerusalem, and Jerusalem would be elevated as a beautiful, high mountain. The borders of Israel would extend much, much farther than they do today, and animals would no longer eat one another. All of these prophecies and more will be fulfilled in the future millennial kingdom. We find out in the last book of the Bible that this kingdom will last 1000 years.

Those of us who will have been raptured and taken to heaven for seven years will return with Jesus to rule and reign with him. We'll have jobs that are exciting, fit our interests and skills, and help Jesus govern the

world with perfect righteousness. There's an old saying that goes, "Find your dream job, and you'll never have to work another day in your life." Your role in the future millennial kingdom will be your dream job—better than a professional YouTuber, better than a professional snowboarder, better than a professional adventure guide, better than a professional white-water rafting instructor, better than anything you could imagine. The best part is we will get to serve Jesus with our talents and abilities for 1000 years in fulfillment of prophecies that currently are more than 2600 years old!

Heaven Forever

After we have ruled and reigned with Jesus in the millennial kingdom, Satan—a fallen angel who rebelled against God and later tempted Adam and Eve, bringing sin into the world—will be released for one last battle. Even though everyone will love and follow Jesus at the beginning of the kingdom, many of the descendants of the original kingdom inhabitants will reject Jesus.

Once Satan is loosed, he will convince many to rebel against God once more. He will lose quickly and miserably, and God will finally put Satan and the people who reject Christ permanently in a place of punishment

the Bible calls the Lake of Fire (Revelation 20:7-15). Evil will be permanently punished, never to return again.

Following this final judgment, God will create a new heaven and earth with a beautiful city called the New Jerusalem! This is where our headquarters will be forever and ever—and it is probably where the living spaces we discussed above will be located as well. In Revelation 21:1-4 we read these amazing words:

> I saw "a new heaven and a new earth," for the first heaven and the first earth had passed away, and there was no longer any sea. I saw the Holy City, the new Jerusalem, coming down out of heaven from God, prepared as a bride beautifully dressed for her husband. And I heard a loud voice from the throne saying, "Look! God's dwelling place is now among the people, and he will dwell with them. They will be his people, and God himself will be with them and be their God. He will wipe every tear from their eyes. There will be no more death or mourning or crying or pain, for the old order of things has passed away."

The rest of Revelation 21 and the first section of Revelation 22 provide many more amazing details about what heaven will be like forever. The New Jerusalem will be made up of amazing precious jewels and have gates made of pearl with giant angels at each gate. It will be a huge 1400-mile cube. God's throne will be there, and his glory will be so bright we won't even need a sun.

Imagine how beautiful it will be with God's bright glory shining through the city of brilliantly colored precious jewels and streets of pure, clear gold. It will be like the most incredible light and fireworks show anyone has ever seen—and it will be like that all the time. There will be no night, and we will never get tired or need to sleep. A beautiful river will flow from God's throne room, and a heavenly, supernatural tree called the tree of life will be there for us to eat from anytime we want. We will enjoy the New Jerusalem and explore the universe on one never-ending, mind-blowing adventure with God.

Think of the best movie you can imagine with all of its computer-generated special effects. Heaven will be 1000 times better, and it will never end. Now, *that's* exciting!

CHAPTER 5

YOUR EXCITING PRESENT!

Heaven is going to be amazing, but so is right now!

GUESS WHAT?

NON-PROPHET

> The thief comes only to steal and kill and destroy;
> I have come that they may have life,
> and have it to the full.
>
> ### JOHN 10:10

One thing we can learn from Bible prophecy is that even when the world seems like it is going crazy, we can have hope, courage, and joy. God is sovereign. That means he is ultimately in control of everything. In Revelation, the final book of the Bible, we can learn about how God will use everything that has happened in the past to bring all things to their final end. God is perfectly fair and completely righteous. He will thoroughly and fairly judge evil, and as we'll see in the section below, he has made a way for everyone to have their sins forgiven if they will humbly turn to Jesus for salvation.

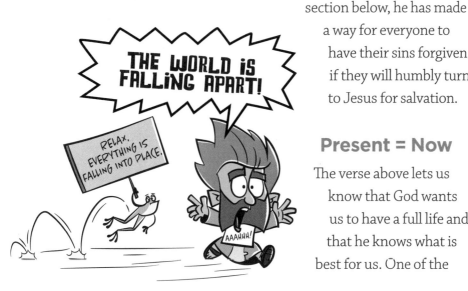

Present = Now

The verse above lets us know that God wants us to have a full life and that he knows what is best for us. One of the

reasons he came was to show us how to truly live. That doesn't mean it will be easy, but it means he will use everything for the good of those who follow him (Romans 8:28). Sadly, a lot of people think God is trying to keep them from blessings. But the opposite is true. He is trying to protect us from harm.

Thinking God was keeping them from something is what got Adam and Eve in trouble in the first place. They could eat from any of the trees of the garden except one—the tree of the knowledge of good and evil. And the enemy tricked them into thinking God was keeping something good from them—so they broke the one rule they had and ate from the tree. This led to all the sin, chaos, and pain that has happened ever since.

God's ways maximize life right now. Obedience always leads to blessing. Disobedience always moves us away from blessing. To live a truly full life now is to live for Jesus. None of us will do it perfectly. It is a journey—but a thrilling one if we follow Jesus and his ways. So how do we do this? What is the starting point? Keep reading and you'll find out!

Present = a Gift

Christians can look forward to a lot of amazing future events, but there's even more good news. Once someone becomes a Christian, their eternal life starts immediately. That doesn't mean they go straight to heaven, but it does mean heaven comes straight to them. The moment someone accepts Jesus as Savior, the Holy Spirit comes to live in them to give guidance and insight.

In the Old Testament, the Holy Spirit came and went according to God's purposes. But now, during the church age, when someone becomes a Christian, the Holy Spirit lives in them and never leaves. Jesus said the Holy Spirit would be our comforter, advocate, or helper. This means God is always with us to help us through anything we face.

paraclete (Greek word) consoler, comforter, helper, advocate, intercessor.

> I will ask the Father, and he will give you another advocate to help you and be with you forever—the Spirit of truth. The world cannot accept him, because it neither sees him nor knows him. But you know him, for he lives with you and will be in you (John 14:16-17).

We serve one God who is three persons—God the Father, God the Son, and God the Holy Spirit. We can't fully understand how God can be three in one, but it is true. I'm one person, but I'm a father, son, and a husband. That is one way to help explain it, but God's mysteries are bigger than we can understand. In Isaiah 55:8-9 God tells us, "'My thoughts are not your thoughts, neither are your ways my ways,' declares the LORD. 'As the heavens are higher than the earth, so are my ways higher than your ways and my thoughts than your thoughts.'"

When Adam and Eve fell, they became sinners, and the law of death and decay entered creation. Sadly, this meant that their fallen nature was passed down to all of us like an inherited trait from our ancient ancestors. Sin is in our DNA, so to speak. It's part of who we are. We're not sinners because we sin. We sin because we're sinners. We're not let

off the hook though, because we each practice sin. We have all know-ingly chosen to do the wrong things at times. We are sinners by nature and by practice.

Our sin has separated us from a holy and pure God. Like oil and water, sin and holiness do not mix. So we have a problem. God can't overlook sin. No matter what we do, we can't work or will our way to God. The separation is too great.

But where there was a problem, God brought a solution. In his unbe-lievable mercy, he sent his sinless Son to pay our sin debt in full. Your sins and mine hung on the cross. The Creator of the universe zipped on some skin and became one of us. Somehow, he was mysteriously fully God and yet fully man. He faced every temptation you or I would ever have—and then some—yet lived a sinless life.

Christ's sinless life, foreshadowed by the spotless lambs that were sacri-ficed under the Old Testament law, was our substitute. Isaiah said that God "laid on him the iniquity of us all" (Isaiah 53:6). We were in debt with no hope of getting out. All of our credit cards were maxed out, and the payment needed far outweighed our ability to even put a dent in it.

But Jesus took our debt for us. He made possible a new beginning. A second chance. A fresh start.

But there's one thing left to complete the transaction. God is a gentleman and never kicks down the door to your free will. A forced gift is no gift at all. We all must make a choice at some point. Will we choose to accept the gift? Or will we leave it there, weighing down the outstretched hands of the grace-filled Gift Giver?

In Revelation 3:20, Jesus said, "Here I am! I stand at the door and knock. If anyone hears my voice and opens the door, I will come in and eat with that person, and they with me." God is relational. Personal. He's not cold and distant. But it's up to you. A relationship is a two-way street. If you haven't already, you need to make a choice. Will you open that door? Will you accept the gift? Will you begin a relationship with the Savior? You can do it right now.

If you have never accepted the Lord's gift of salvation, now is the time. I plead with you to ask Jesus to be your Savior. It's not a matter of how good you are; it's a matter of how good he is. He took all your sin on himself at the cross. You can't be good enough. Only he can. He died as your substitute. He took the rap for you—but you must place your faith in him.

> # But God demonstrates his own love for us in this: while we were still sinners, Christ died for us.
> ## Romans 5:8

This is not a scare tactic, but I truly believe time is short. The converging signs point to a soon-returning King and an even sooner rapture. Even if I'm wrong, we are not guaranteed our next breath. If accepting Christ is something you want to do, here's how. It's very simple, but people often make it too complex. One does not become a Christian by following a formula, but I've found that what I'm about to share is an effective way to explain what it means to receive Christ and become a true Christian. It's so simple a child can understand it. It's as simple as A, B, C.

Admit that you are a sinner. None of us are perfect. We all fall short. Romans 3:23 says, "All have sinned and fall short of the glory of God." And Romans 6:23 adds, "The wages [payment] of sin is death, but the gift of God is eternal life in Christ Jesus our Lord."

Believe that Jesus is God's Son and that he died on the cross with your sins on him. "While we were still sinners, Christ died for us" (Romans 5:8).

Confess him as your Lord. This doesn't mean you will never mess up again. Rather, it means you will serve him and learn his ways as you grow spiritually. "If you confess with your mouth the Lord Jesus and believe in your heart that God has raised Him from the dead, you will be saved" (Romans 10:9 NKJV).

Here's a simple prayer you can pray. These words aren't magic. Again, this is not a formula. But if these words accurately reflect the motives of your heart, then when you pray this prayer, you will become a Christian. You will have placed your faith in Christ and will have had your sins forgiven. You will look forward to an eternity with Jesus in heaven, and you will avoid the terrible time of tribulation that will soon come to the world. Pray this prayer now.

PRAY THIS PRAYER
iF YOU WANT TO ACCEPT JESUS!

"Lord Jesus, I admit that I am a sinner. I have sinned against you, and sin separates me from you. I thank you that you died on the cross for me. You took my sins upon you and paid my penalty at the cross. I believe you are who you say you are—God in the flesh. I believe you died for my sins. I want to accept your gift of salvation and, at this moment, I ask you to be my Savior. I thank you for this great forgiveness. I now have new life. I now claim you as my Savior and my Lord. In Jesus's name, amen."

sign your name here if you prayed this prayer!

add the date so you will always remember

If you just prayed that prayer, you are a new creation. The Bible tells us that heaven is celebrating right now because of your decision. The Holy Spirit now indwells you and will guide you and keep you. You won't be perfect, but you are forgiven, and he will never leave you. His work in you has just begun. You are an adopted co-heir with Christ. You will one day live and reign with him in the millennial kingdom and forever in eternity. Welcome to the family of God!

If you have not accepted Christ because you have doubts, questions, or reservations, that's okay, but don't leave them there. Please investigate them fully. Also, I dare you to pray this prayer: "God, if you are the God of the Bible and Jesus is the Son of God, please open my eyes and help me believe. I want to know truth wherever it may lead."

Conclusion

Now that you have read this entire book, I think you see why Bible prophecy is so important. Through Bible prophecy we learn God's magnificent plan to redeem mankind—to pay what we owe so that we don't have to. From the first book of the Bible to the last, God's incredible story is told to us so we can know what to do. Fulfilled Bible prophecy proves that the Bible is from God and that we can trust what it says about the things we can't prove—such as the amazing events that will happen in the future, or the truth that God the Holy Spirit comes to live inside of us when we accept Jesus as our Savior. I hope you have enjoyed this journey with me, the Non-Prophet, and my pet frog, Plague. We hope to see you again soon!

NOTES

1. What Is Bible Prophecy?

1. Jewish Virtual Library, "Population of Israel/Palestine," https://www.jewishvirtuallibrary.org/population-of-israel-palestine-1553-present.

2. Mark Twain, *The Innocents Abroad* (Hartford, CN: American Publishing, 1869).

2. Why Is Bible Prophecy Important?

3. Dave Roos, "Lewis and Clark's Travels Included Dozens of Astonishing Animal Encounters," *History*, https://www.history.com/news/lewis-and-clark-animals-american-west.

ABOUT THE AUTHOR

TODD HAMPSON is a speaker, illustrator, animation producer, and the bestselling author of The Non-Prophet's Guide™ book series. His award-winning animation company, Timbuktoons, has produced content for many well-known ministry organizations. Todd and his wife are the proud parents of three grown children and make their home in Georgia.

toddhampson.com

To learn more about Harvest House books and
to read sample chapters, visit our website:

www.HarvestHousePublishers.com

HARVEST HOUSE PUBLISHERS
EUGENE, OREGON